Jane Goodall

Protector of Chimpanzees

Jane Goodall
Protector of Chimpanzees

Virginia Meachum

Enslow Publishers, Inc.

44 Fadem Road   PO Box 38
Box 699   Aldershot
Springfield, NJ 07081   Hants GU12 6BP
USA   UK

Library of Congress Cataloging-in-Publication Data

Meachum, Virginia.
    Jane Goodall, protector of chimpanzees / Virginia Meachum.
        p.   cm. — (People to know)
    Includes bibliographical references (p.   ) and index.
    Summary: Explores the life and research of the English animal
behaviorist who undertook the first long-term study of chimpanzees
in the wild.
    ISBN 0-89490-827-8
    1. Goodall, Jane, 1934–   —Juvenile literature. 2. Primatologists—
England—Biography—Juvenile literature. 3. Chimpanzees—Tanzania—
Gombe Stream National Park—Juvenile literature. [1. Goodall,
Jane, 1934– . 2. Chimpanzees. 3. Zoologists. 4. Women—Biography.]
I. Title. II. Series.
QL31.G58M43 1997
590'.92—dc21
[B]   97-2881
                                                CIP
                                                AC

Printed in the United States of America

10 9 8 7 6 5 4 3 2

Illustration Credits:
AP/Wide World Photos, pp. 63, 71; Baron Hugo Van Lawick/National
Geographic Image Collection, pp. 9, 40, 52, 55, 66, 68; Bournemouth
Tourism, p. 14; Chicago Tribune, p. 89; Chicago Zoological Society
Audiovisual Services, Photo by Mike Greer, pp. 23, 26, 45; Corbis-Bettmann,
pp. 12, 19; Courtesy Department of Library Services, No. 326466, — Rota,
American Museum of Natural History, p. 31; © M. Steward/Globe Photos,
p. 6; © Michael Neugebauer/Globe Photos, p. 67; © Newell-Smith/Globe
Photos, p. 34; UPI/Corbis-Bettmann, pp. 74, 84.

Cover Illustration: Ken Regan/Camera 5

Contents

Jane Goodall

A Time of Terror

In the summer of 1960, a delicate-looking young woman with ponytailed blond hair and a pack on her back was trying to observe a group of wild chimpanzees in the jungle of the Gombe Stream Game Reserve. Jane Goodall had been sent to Tanzania, in East Africa, by anthropologist Dr. Louis S. B. Leakey, curator of the National Museum of Natural History in Nairobi. Her mission was to observe and take notes on the behavior of wild chimpanzees. No one had ever before made a successful study of this great ape in its natural environment.

The chimpanzee is our closest living relative. Nearly 99 percent of chimpanzees' genetic makeup

(DNA) is identical to the genetic makeup of humans. Their brains are more like ours than any other living creatures' are.[1]

Early each morning, day after day, Jane Goodall climbed the mountain near her tent camp to reach a peak that offered a view of the tropical forest down in the valley. Here she sat all day, observing the chimps through her binoculars. They came to feed on the ripened fruit in the trees of the valley.

Each time the chimps spotted her, they vanished into the trees of the forest. One day she decided to move down the mountain slope and venture into that dense forest. Quietly she threaded her way through shoulder-high grass and tangled undergrowth, searching for a group of chimps. She had heard their hooting calls not too long before.

Suddenly, a few yards ahead, the huge black form of an adult chimpanzee appeared. Goodall stopped at once and remained still. All was eerily quiet for the moment. Then a low hoo sounded on her right. Another hoo came from within the tree directly above her head. Glancing up, she saw a large male glaring down. He shook a branch, threatening. From the tall grass behind came a deep hoo, nervously repeated over and over. Goodall was surrounded.

Agitated chimp calls from among the branches grew louder. She dropped to the ground. Trying to appear uninterested, she pretended to chew on some leaves and twigs. At once the male chimp above her screamed a long drawn-out wraaaa—an alarming, savage sound. Several large males rushed out of hiding, stamping the ground, screaming, and shaking tree branches. One chimp of great size and strength, his long black hair bristling in a show of anger, charged directly toward her. Jane crouched on the ground. At the last second, he veered off. Then, quite suddenly, the screaming stopped. All was quiet. The performance had ended. The entire group of chimpanzees plodded silently on.

Goodall's legs were shaking as she slowly stood up. She could have been torn to pieces. Although a

All was quiet in the jungle. Then Jane Goodall heard a low, threatening hoo, followed by a savage screaming sound. Goodall was surrounded.

male chimp stands only four feet tall, he weighs about one hundred pounds, and his strength is at least three times greater than that of a grown man.[2]

Yet this terrifying experience did not discourage her. It merely became another observation—an anecdote—to be written up and added to her daily notes. Goodall was living her childhood dream—that of going to Africa and working with wild animals. No matter how frustrating or hazardous the conditions, she would never give up.

Now, decades after this experience, Dr. Jane Goodall is known worldwide for her contributions to the study of animal behavior. She was the first person to undertake a long-term study of wild chimpanzees in their natural environment. Her findings have provided important discoveries, not only for students of primate behavior, but also for anthropologists, medical scientists, naturalists, and others.

What could have prompted this childhood dream that has served so many?

An Early Start

Jane Goodall was born in London, England, on April 3, 1934. Her father, Mortimer Goodall, was an engineer whose hobby was auto-racing. Her mother, Myfanwe Joseph Goodall (known to everyone as Vanne), was a writer as well as a homemaker. Judy, Jane's sister, was born four years later.

For Jane's second birthday, her parents gave her a toy chimpanzee, Jubilee, named after the first chimp ever born in the London Zoo. Jane cherished this life-like toy chimp with its silky hair and brown eyes. It was as tall as she was at the time and accompanied her everywhere. Jubilee was her first encounter with the ape family, but it would not be her last.

The Goodall family lived in the London area until Jane was five years old. Then they moved to Bournemouth, a popular seaside resort town on the coast of the English Channel. Here, they shared a house with Jane's maternal grandmother, Danny; two aunts; and an uncle, a senior consultant surgeon at a London hospital who came home on weekends. The large brick Victorian house with a vast garden, enclosed by a tall, thick hedge, was called the Birches. This would be Jane's home throughout her childhood.

At this time, dictator Adolf Hitler, the Nazi party

A chimpanzee was the biggest attraction at the London Zoo in the 1930s. At the age of two, Jane was given a toy chimpanzee, Jubilee, named after the first chimp born in the London Zoo.

leader, and his German Army had begun an invasion of Poland, which also threatened Great Britain. England declared war on Germany on September 3, 1939, and Jane's father enlisted in the British Army to help fight the enemy.

During 1940 and 1941, the German Air Force bombed London day and night, forcing people to seek refuge in subway stations and underground shelters. Precautions were taken at Bournemouth also. An air-raid shelter was installed in the house, where the family gathered whenever an air-raid warning sounded. Food, clothing, and gasoline were all rationed because most of these items were needed by the men and women defending England. After the United States joined England in fighting against the Nazis in December 1941, Jane remembers seeing American soldiers stationed near the Birches, waiting to go to the battlefront in France, Holland, and Belgium.

In 1942, when Jane was eight years old, her parents were divorced. She continued to live in Bournemouth with her mother and sister.

Jane started her schooling in kindergarten, and continued on through the equivalent of our senior high school. Although she did well in her schoolwork, Jane longed for the weekends and summer holidays when she could be outdoors. From a very early age, she was fascinated with all kinds of wildlife—insects, birds, squirrels—and was immensely curious about their lives. When eighteen months old, she was discovered taking earthworms to bed with her to watch how they walked without legs. Her mother explained, "Jane, if you leave them here they'll be dead soon, because they need the earth."[1] At once, the young naturalist carried them outdoors.

Jane always seemed to be searching for answers. Another well-remembered incident took place when she was about four and a half. The family frequently spent time at her paternal grandparents' manor house out in the country, with cows in the fields nearby and a large enclosure for the hens and henhouses. Given a basket and assigned to collect the hens' eggs each day, Jane soon wanted to know where an egg came out of a hen. Determined to find out, she crawled into a hot, stuffy henhouse, crouched down in the straw, and silently waited for a hen to come in.

Jane Goodall grew up in Bournemouth, England, a resort town on the English Channel. Shown here are the beach and pier at Bournemouth.

Four hours later, Jane finally did get to watch a hen strut to its nest and lay an egg. Bursting with excitement, she crawled out of the henhouse and ran all the way to the manor house to break the news. Meanwhile, Mrs. Goodall, having searched for her little girl for hours, was just about to call the police. Then, however, instead of scolding her, Jane recalls, "She saw the excitement and sat down to hear this wonderful story."[2]

At the Birches, Jane spent a lot of time exploring outdoors, but in the winter she was content to stay indoors, curled up by the fire, reading. She particularly liked books about animals—*The Jungle Book* by Rudyard Kipling, the Tarzan books by Edgar Rice Burroughs—but *The Story of Doctor Doolittle* by Hugh Lofting captured her interest most of all. Over and over again she read about the Englishman who talked with animals in Africa. "I know that I started wanting to be in Africa when I read Dr. Doolittle. I think I was about seven at that time."[3]

Although Jane wanted to see and study the wild animals she read about, there was not even a zoo nearby. She had to content herself with watching and studying the wild creatures inhabiting the large garden of the Birches. This was done with amazing dedication. She collected a wide variety of pets— snails, turtles, guinea pigs, and others—to watch how they behaved, and she wrote notes on everything she observed. Her mother recalls that Jane was "happy for hours in the garden watching spiders or beetles or worms and making notes. She was almost literally born with a pencil in her hand and she started recording everything as soon as she could write."[4]

At one time, Jane started the Alligator Club, a nature club consisting of four members—Jane; her sister, Judy; and two houseguests, Sally and Sue, who came for summer holidays. They went on nature walks and wrote down notes about the insects and birds they saw. Then Jane would identify the creatures from reference books in the home library. In the fall, she put together an Alligator Club magazine filled with drawings of insects, animal quizzes, and stories. The other members were supposed to contribute also, but it seemed that only their club leader was dedicated to this project.

As Jane grew older, she went every Saturday to a riding school in the country. In exchange for extra riding lessons, she learned how to care for the horses and ponies—grooming and feeding them and cleaning the saddles and bridles, which had to be washed every day and rubbed with saddle soap.

When she was fourteen, Jane was allowed to take clients out for rides and sometimes rode in horse shows. One time she even participated in a fox hunt, not thinking about what it really meant. In fox hunting, a popular sport in England, hunters on horseback follow a pack of hounds in pursuit of a fox. These hounds have been trained to hunt foxes by following the foot scent of the fox on the ground.

For Jane, the excitement of jumping hedges and the challenge of keeping up with the other riders was a heady experience—that is, until she saw the exhausted fox caught and thrown to the hounds to be torn up. "Then I felt sick, and the excitement of the hunt was gone. I never went hunting again."[5]

Of all the animals in Jane's childhood, a dog named Rusty seems to have made a lasting impression. He ate and slept at the local hotel, where his owners lived, but spent his days tagging along with Jane. They met one day when she was exercising a neighbor's dog on a run along the beach, and having found her, Rusty showed up every morning at her front door—not to be fed but to share her company.

Jane taught him to shake hands, to sit and beg for a treat, to shut the door, to jump through a hoop, and other tricks. He was a willing learner, and she was an appreciative teacher. In turn, Jane learned much about animal behavior from Rusty. "He taught me that dogs can think things out—that they can reason."[6]

As always, Jane was reluctant to see the outdoor summer holiday end and another indoor school year begin. She attended Uplands school at Parkstone, a private school near Bournemouth, and did quite well in the subjects that interested her—English, history, biology, and Scripture. Languages and math were more difficult, and meant she must work harder to come in second or third in scholarship at the end of the term. Jane and her best friend, Marie-Claude Mange, known as Clo, usually alternated coming in second or third place.

Jane was eighteen when she graduated from high school. What would she do next? Jane knew what she really wanted to do—observe and write about wild animals—but how could she make a living doing that?

Yearning

B_y the fall of 1952, Jane Goodall had decided to enroll in a secretarial school in London. This was far removed from studying animals, but as she explained in an interview many years later, "Mum said secretaries could get jobs anywhere in the world, and I still knew my destiny lay in Africa."[1] So she learned to type, take shorthand, and do bookkeeping.

Attending school in London was a new experience. When not in class or studying, she visited art galleries and the London Zoo, and attended concerts and the theater (choosing the least expensive seats, as she had very little money).

Upon earning her secretary's diploma, Goodall

returned to Bournemouth and worked in a children's clinic. The clinic was run by her Aunt Olwen Joseph (known as Olly), who was a physiotherapist. Similar to a physical therapist, a physiotherapist is a person qualified to treat a physical disability or pain by using such physical techniques as exercise, massage, hydrotherapy, and so on. The clinic treated children of all ages for almost any kind of physical disability. Babies with birth defects such as clubfeet, polio sufferers with paralyzed limbs, brain-damaged children, and patients in braces or in wheelchairs were among

In the fall of 1952, Goodall enrolled in a secretarial school in London. She studied typing, shorthand, and bookkeeping.

those being treated. Several times a week doctors came in to examine their individual patients, and Goodall would do whatever typing the doctors needed.

After six months at the clinic, she accepted a job in the city of Oxford. Located about fifty miles northwest of London on the River Thames, it is the home of Oxford University, the oldest university in England. Goodall worked in the filing department in the administrative building of the university and lived in a house with several Oxford graduate students. This living arrangement put her in touch with other students and their university-related activities. She attended the famous May ball at Oxford, but more in keeping with her love of nature was the time she spent on the Thames. In the early morning or late evening, she would take out a canoe and quietly paddle along, observing the swans, moorhens, and other water birds. Rowing was another of Goodall's activities, and she also learned to punt. In punting, a small, flat-bottomed boat is driven forward by lifting a long pole out of the water, then pushing it down hard in the riverbed to move the boat along.

After a year at Oxford, Goodall moved back to London to work in a film studio that made documentary films. Her job was to choose music for the films, but she also learned how to edit and make sound tracks, and was introduced to a number of other techniques used in filmmaking.

While working at the studio, Goodall lived in her father's apartment. Although her parents were divorced, they remained good friends. This was an opportunity for father and daughter to spend some time together in London.

By now Goodall had experienced three different kinds of work, but none was the work she dreamed of doing—studying the wild animals of Africa in their natural environment. Meanwhile, she continued to read books about African animals and spent many hours at the Natural History Museum studying the wild animal exhibits. Would her dream ever come true?

During this period of filling in time and of yearning, much of Goodall's conviction that she would reach her dream came from Vanne Goodall, who understood and encouraged her daughter. About her mother, Goodall has said, "When I was growing up, whatever I wanted to do, providing it was something remotely sensible, she would back me up. She always would say, 'If you want to do something enough, you'll find a way to do it.'"[2] Before long, "a way" did seem to be opening up.

One morning, she received a letter from her high school friend Clo. The letter was quite unexpected, as they had lost touch with each other during the past few years. Clo's parents had just bought a farm in Kenya, Africa, and she invited Goodall to come and visit her in Kenya. Of course she would go!

Goodall's goal now would be to earn enough money to pay for the long ocean journey to and from Africa. Since her salary at the film studio was quite small, she believed she could earn more in wages and tips working as a waitress. Resigning from her studio job, Goodall returned to the Birches and became a waitress in the dining room of a nearby hotel. She had to learn many new skills in order to become a good waitress, and she carefully saved her weekly earnings. In less than a year, she had saved enough to purchase a round-trip ticket for passage to Africa.

Jane Goodall was twenty-three years old when she boarded an ocean liner for the twenty-one day voyage to Kenya. The ship sailed along the west coast of Africa, around the Cape of Good Hope, and up to Mombasa, the coastal port of Kenya.

Arriving at Mombasa, Goodall then boarded a train for a two-day journey to Nairobi, the capital of Kenya. Here she was met by Clo, who drove her over a dirt road to the farm. Along the way, Goodall had her first close-up view of a giraffe. It stood in the middle of the road, towering above the car and looking down at them. Then it turned and slowly ran away. It was a revealing moment for Goodall. Now she knew that she had actually arrived in the Africa of her dreams.

Jane Goodall stayed with Clo and her family for three weeks, and then moved to Nairobi to begin a new job. Before leaving England, she had made arrangements with a large British company for temporary work at its branch office in Kenya. Her purpose was to earn enough money to support herself while trying to find a way to work with animals.

Before long, an acquaintance who learned of her plan suggested that she make an appointment to meet Dr. Louis S. B. Leakey, a noted anthropologist and paleontologist who was the curator of what is now the National Museum of Natural History in

In Kenya, Goodall had her first close-up view of a giraffe. She knew then that she had arrived in the Africa of her dreams.

Nairobi. An anthropologist studies the origin of early humans—their physical, social, and cultural development and their behavior. A paleontologist studies fossils—bones, stone tools, leaf imprints, footprints— from prehistoric times. Dr. Leakey worked in both of these sciences.

Upon interviewing Goodall, Dr. Leakey was apparently impressed with how much she knew about African animals. He immediately offered her a job as an assistant secretary. It was a lucky break. Now she could stay in Africa and work among a staff of museum naturalists, learning from them as she worked.

Another lucky break came even before Goodall's work began at the museum. Dr. Leakey and his wife, Mary Leakey, took Goodall and another woman museum worker on their annual expedition to Olduvai Gorge on the plains of Serengeti National Park. In prehistoric times, Olduvai was the site of a large lake around which early humans once lived and animals came in search of water. At the time of Goodall's visit in 1957, this was a secluded area in northwestern Tanzania, known to very few white people. Every summer the Leakeys drove their Land Rover over the unmarked trail to dig for fossils.

After a three-day journey, they arrived at Olduvai and set up camp for the summer. Later a truck arrived, bringing more equipment and an African field staff to help with the digging. Each morning they all dug for fossils under the hot African sun. Picks and shovels were used to remove the topsoil. Then, hunting knives were used to chip away the harder soil in the search for bones. Dental picks were used to free the fossils without damaging them. The finds were then sorted, numbered, and carefully stored. Later they would be taken to the museum in Nairobi for a final cleaning.

In the evening, when the work was finished, Goodall and her young woman co-worker would wander off to explore this remote, wild area. Once they came upon a black rhinocerous and escaped being noticed by it only because rhinos are shortsighted. Two-horned and thick-skinned, a rhino is one of the largest land creatures. Its long front horn, sometimes over three feet long, is used for attacking and for overturning bushes and small trees so it can feed on their leaves. A rhino is usually quiet and harmless, but if confused or angered by other animals or humans, it may charge and attack ferociously. Another evening, while tramping through the gorge, they were startled to hear a growl. A young male lion stood watching them from only a short distance away. They began to walk across the gorge slowly, for they knew that lions chase animals that run away. For a time, the lion followed them. Then, suddenly, he stopped and disappeared into the vegetation.[3] The two women climbed out of the gorge onto the open plain and returned safely to camp. These scary encounters never seemed to dim Goodall's eagerness to learn more about wild animals.

When the summer was over, she worked all day in Dr. Leakey's office and lived in one of the staff apartments. Here, among people who shared her interest in animals, she began to acquire an assortment of orphaned or mistreated animals. Among them was a

While exploring in Olduvai Gorge, Goodall and a co-worker came upon a black rhinoceros. They avoided being discovered only because rhinos are shortsighted.

vervet monkey—a long-tailed African monkey distinguished by a rusty patch at the base of its tail. Other animals included a dwarf mongoose, a hedgehog, and a bush baby. The bush baby (also known as a galago) had come first, and soon became an office resident. Small, bushy-tailed, with large eyes and ears and woolly fur, a bush baby makes a wailing sound similar to a baby crying. Levi, as he was named, slept during the day in a gourd in Dr. Leakey's office, occasionally waking up and jumping uninvited onto someone's shoulders. At night he leaped about catching insects.

Although Goodall found her work at the museum

and her expedition to Olduvai Gorge fascinating, her childhood dream was still unfulfilled. She needed to find a way to work with wild animals in their natural environment. "I wanted to come as close to talking to animals as I could—to be like Doctor Doolittle."[4]

In Dr. Leakey's ongoing search for the remains of our prehistoric ancestors, he believed that a study of chimpanzees might provide some insight into the behavior of early humans. For some time he had been interested in learning about a group of chimpanzees living in the Gombe Stream Game Reserve, near the eastern shore of Lake Tanganyika in northern Tanzania. Only one man, Professor Henry W. Nissen, had previously attempted a serious study of chimpanzees in the wild, but for only two and a half months. Dr. Leakey had in mind a study of at least two years, and possibly ten. He spoke of the patience and dedication that the person making such a long-term study of these wild chimpanzees would need.

Jane Goodall had no college degree and no formal research training, but to study chimpanzees in the wild was exactly the kind of work she had always wanted to do. One day she told Dr. Leakey so.

He replied, "Why do you think I'm talking about them?"[5]

It didn't matter to him that she had little experience and no degree. "He wanted someone whose mind was uncluttered and unbiased by theory who would make the study for no other reason than a real desire for knowledge; and, in addition, someone with a sympathetic understanding of animals," Goodall later explained.[6] Of course, she accepted.

Now Dr. Leakey needed to do the important work of raising the necessary funds for this project. Meanwhile, he advised Goodall to return to London and learn all she could about chimpanzees. She arrived home a little more than a year after leaving on her first trip to Africa. How soon she would return remained uncertain.

Learning

$\mathbf{W}$ith her need to learn all that she could about chimpanzees, Jane Goodall was fortunate to find work at the London Zoo. She did not work directly with animals but as a librarian in the documentary film unit. A few times, however, she was allowed to drive the young orangutans to filming sessions and, in that contact, learned something about them. "It was so much fun to have Alex in my tiny car, and see people's faces when they noticed. That was when I learned how wonderfully gentle young orangs are."[1]

Every day when off duty, she visited the caged chimpanzees. She brought them such treats as strawberries, blackberries, or peas in their pods and spent hours observing them. Seeing these wild animals shut up in their small cages, Jane vowed that one day she would try to help chimps in zoos have better lives.[2]

To prepare for her future months of field study among chimpanzees, Goodall read everything she could find about this particular member of the ape family. The ape family includes the four kinds of animals most like man—the gorilla, the chimpanzee, the orangutan, and the gibbon.

Their bodies are much like those of humans, with similar bones, nerves, muscles, and other organs, but their arms are longer and legs shorter than those of a human.

The chimpanzee, like the other apes, has on each foot a big toe that looks like a thumb. This enables it to use both its hands and its feet as skillfully as humans use their hands. A chimpanzee can hold fruit in its feet as well as in its hands, and can grasp branches with both its hands and its feet when swinging by its arms from tree branch to branch. Chimpanzees walk on all fours, placing the backs of their fingers and knuckles against the ground. This is called knuckle-walking.[3]

Except for their hands, feet, and faces, chimpanzees are covered with lank black hair. Like all apes, chimpanzees do not have tails. Also, chimps cannot swim, and they do not like to get their feet wet. They will swing through trees or leap over a stream to avoid wading through it.

These were the apes that Jane Goodall would be observing in the Gombe Stream Game Reserve (now known as Gombe National Park) on Lake Tanganyika

Chimps are covered with lank black hair, except on their hands, feet, and faces.

in Tanzania. The narrow, two-mile strip of beach, dense forests, and twenty-five-hundred-foot mountains, stretching about ten miles along the eastern shore of the lake, totaled about thirty square miles. The reserve was home to about one hundred and sixty wild chimpanzees.

Leakey's search for someone to finance this long-term field study did not go smoothly. There was doubt among some colleagues that the study of great apes was relevant to the understanding of our prehistoric ancestors, and there was further doubt about his choice of Jane Goodall, a young woman with no academic qualifications, to perform the study.[4]

Finally, the Wilkie Foundation of Des Plaines, Illinois—an organization that sponsors studies of humans and other primates—agreed to give Goodall a grant for a three-month field study at Gombe. The grant was later extended to six months.

Another problem was in gaining permission for the study from government officials in Tanganyika, which in 1960 was under British rule. (Tanganyika became independent in 1961 and became Tanzania when it merged with Zanzibar in 1964.) The British officials did not feel it was safe for a young, single woman to go into the wilds of Africa to study animals by herself. She had to choose a companion. Goodall chose her adventurous mother.

Late in the spring of 1960, the two women flew to Nairobi, where they assembled their camping gear—tents, bedding, cooking utensils, and canned food. They also took binoculars, notebooks for recording observations, and drab-colored clothing so Jane could blend into the landscape.

They were all set for the three-day motor trip to Kigoma, the largest town in the Gombe area, when word came of trouble among the African fishermen on the beaches of the reserve. They could not safely go until the area game ranger, David Anstey, had settled the problem. During this delay, Leakey arranged for Goodall to make a trial study of the vervet monkeys on Lolui Island in Lake Victoria.

The two Goodalls went by train to Lake Victoria, where a motor launch captained by Hassan and his assistant, both Africans, brought them to the island for a three-week study. Hassan had worked for Dr. Leakey for many years. The boat, anchored near the island, was their temporary home. Each morning Hassan rowed Goodall ashore, where she remained all day, watching the wild monkeys and taking notes. Evenings, he rowed her back to the boat for a simple camp supper with her mother and a night of being lulled to sleep by the gently rocking boat.

Almost four weeks later, a radio message recalled them to Nairobi. The study of vervet monkeys had taught Goodall some things about note-taking, what kinds of clothes to wear in the field, and what movements a wild monkey would tolerate in an observer. All of this would be helpful in starting her work at Gombe.

Returning to Nairobi, the Goodalls now set off on the eight-hundred-mile journey to Kigoma. Dr. Bernard Verdcourt, director of the East African Herbarium, had offered to drive them in his Land

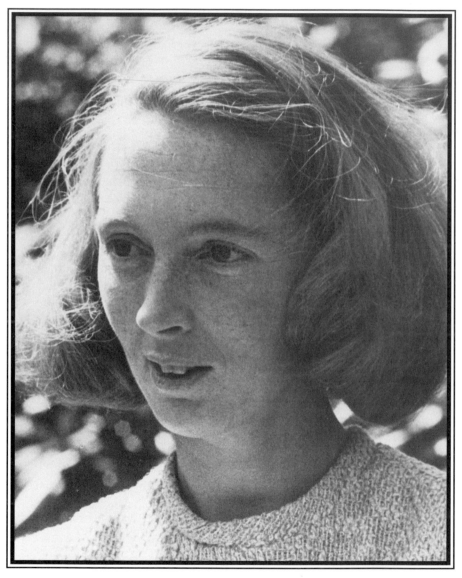

As a young, single woman, Jane Goodall was not permitted by British officials to go into the African jungle by herself to study animals. She would have to choose a companion.

Rover. (A herbarium is a museum where dried plants are collected and arranged for study and display.)

After three days of travel over dusty roads, often through woodlands infested with tsetse flies—gray bloodsucking insects—they arrived at Kigoma. Here they were delayed once more. Violence had broken out in the Belgian Congo (now Zaire) on the other side of Lake Tanganyika, and Kigoma was overflowing with boatloads of Belgian refugees. The district commissioner explained that there was no chance of the women going on to the Gombe Reserve. They must wait to find out how the local Africans would react to the rioting in the Congo. During the wait, they booked a room at one of the town's only two hotels. Here they slept and stored their bulky camping equipment.

With more and more refugees arriving, the town was vastly overcrowded. Temporary housing in the local warehouse was arranged, where refugees slept on mattresses or blankets lined up on the cement floor. Goodall and her mother volunteered their help, making hundreds of sandwiches and serving drinks to the crowd lining up for food. Two days later, when most of the refugees had been carried by extra trains to Dar es Salaam, Tanganyika's capital, the Goodalls were still not permitted to leave for Gombe. David Anstey, the game ranger, had not yet succeeded in sorting out the trouble between the fishermen on the shores of Gombe.

The two women filled their days getting acquainted with this small African town, since this was where they would be coming every few weeks for supplies. Most of the activity was down along the harbor. Here on Lake Tanganyika, boats came from Burundi, Zambia, Malawi, and the Congo. The administrative offices, police station, post office, and railway station were all located near the harbor. The one main street ran upward through the main part of Kigoma, shaded by mango trees and lined on either side with tiny shops. The market at the main square was filled with a colorful array of bananas, oranges, purple passion fruit, assorted vegetables, and bottles of red cooking oil made from the fruit of oil nut palms.

During the delay, they hired an African cook, Dominic Charles, who would accompany them to Gombe. They also bought a small gift, which Anstey had suggested they do, to present to the village leader, whom they would meet upon reaching the reserve.

The women had been in Kigoma for more than a week when they were finally given permission to go on to the Gombe Stream Reserve. Goodall had almost given up hope of ever seeing a chimpanzee. At last they were aboard the government launch that had been lent to them for transporting their equipment, including their twelve-foot dinghy. Regarding this expedition, Goodall has written, "I can remember looking down into the incredibly clear water and thinking to myself, I expect the boat will sink, or I shall fall overboard and be eaten by a crocodile."[5] Luck was with them. There were no more delays.

A Dream
Come True

The trip north from Kigoma to Gombe was a twelve-mile journey on long, narrow Lake Tanganyika. This lake, the longest freshwater lake in the world, is fed from streams flowing down the steep mountains behind its shoreline. From their launch, Goodall and her mother could see fishing villages along the mountain slopes and in the valleys—clusters of simple mud and grass huts and an occasional larger building roofed with corrugated steel. Fishermen's canoes lined the shore inside a series of bays along the lake. When they had traveled about seven miles, David Anstey pointed out the southern boundary of the Gombe Stream Reserve. Here the mountains were thickly wooded, sloping into valleys of dense, tropical forests. A number of fishermen's huts could be seen at intervals along the beaches of the reserve. Anstey explained that these were temporary dwellings for those Africans who had permits to fish and to dry their catch on the reserve beaches during the dry season, which stretches from about mid-May to mid-October. During the rainy season, they returned to their homes beyond the boundaries of the reserve.

Two hours after leaving Kigoma, the launch dropped anchor at Kasekela village, headquarters of the two government game scouts who were responsible for protecting the thirty-square-mile Gombe Reserve. It was also home to the few Africans who had permission to live permanently on the reserve so the scouts would not be totally isolated. A group had gathered on the beach to watch the arrival of the white woman who had come to Gombe to study the chimpanzees.

Jane Goodall was twenty-six years old. Slender and delicate looking, her long blond hair pulled back in a ponytail, she had come to Africa to study wild animals. She had come to fulfill her childhood dream.

It was July 16, 1960, when Goodall, along with Vanne Goodall, David Anstey, and Dominic Charles, stepped from the dinghy onto the sandy shore at Gombe. They were greeted first by the scouts, and then by the honorary headman of the village. This white-bearded, red-turbaned figure, dressed in a red coat over white flowing robes, gave a long welcoming speech in Swahili, the predominant language in East Africa. At that time, Goodall understood only fragments of what he said. She then presented him with the small gift that she had bought in Kigoma.

After the ceremony, Anstey led the newcomers about thirty yards away from the beach, down a narrow path through thick vegetation to a small clearing near the gurgling Kakombe Stream. Shaded by tall oil nut palms, this would be their campsite. Anstey and the two African scouts set up the large army tent that Goodall and her mother would share. Then, down on the beach under some trees, they helped set up a tent for Dominic Charles.

The two women quickly unpacked their camping gear—cots, bedding, clothing, a couple of tin plates and mugs, eating utensils, and other necessities. It was now late afternoon, and Goodall slipped away to explore. She climbed the nearby mountain slope until she was high enough to look down on the lake and a lush green valley. The valley was where she planned to look for chimpanzees the next day. On the way up the mountain, she had seen a bushbuck—an African antelope with spiraling horns. He stopped, stared, then bounded away. She also encountered a troop of about sixty baboons. They were obviously alarmed by this strange white creature. Some of them climbed trees, shook the branches threateningly, and barked loudly. Goodall remained undaunted, and the troop soon moved on. Recalling this incident in a later interview, she said, "I met a troop of barking baboons and knew then that my dream had come true."[1]

Goodall returned to camp to find Dominic cooking their supper over an open fire. They would have the fresh food they brought from Kigoma for only a few

A small clearing, shaded by tall oil nut palms, became the campsite for Jane Goodall and her mother. Shown here are Jane and a local fisherman.

days, as they had no refrigerator. From then on they would be eating canned meat and vegetables, which Dominic would sometimes make into a stew. He would also bake bread for them in a pit oven.

After supper, mother and daughter sat around the campfire quietly talking before retiring to their camp cots. That first night, Goodall pulled her cot outside their tent to sleep under the gently rustling fronds of a palm tree.

In the morning, Goodall was eager to begin looking for chimpanzees, but this was not to be. A rumor had spread that she was a government spy, and a number of the local Africans were worried.[2] They couldn't believe this white woman had come all the way from England only to look at apes. To calm their fears, Anstey had arranged for several of the locals to come that day to meet Goodall and her mother.

Another setback occurred when Anstey informed Goodall that she was not to travel around the mountains alone, except near camp. He had arranged for two of the game scouts to accompany her, one as a porter to carry her haversack (a single-strapped bag worn over one shoulder, used for carrying supplies). Goodall had believed the way to gain the trust of wild chimpanzees was to move about alone, but the two scouts were assigned to ensure her safety. Roaming through the forests were fierce wild buffalo and meat-eating leopards; even the chimpanzees could be dangerous.

The following morning, Goodall and her two companions, Adolf and Rashidi, who would be her porter, set off for Mitumba Valley, where Adolf had reported seeing chimpanzees the day before. They followed along the side of a shallow stream, among the giant trees of the rain forest. Tiny lizards slid down tree trunks, and woody vines, called lianas, climbed up the trees and hung from sturdy branches above. More than a hundred feet above the ground, the spreading tree foliage formed a canopy over the forest, shutting out most of the sunlight. Forest birds trilled and chirped, and redtail monkeys leaped about high in the trees.

Before long, Adolf led them up the side of the valley, where walking upright through the vine-tangled undergrowth was difficult. At last he brought them to an enormous msulula tree laden with small orange and red fruit. It was evident that chimpanzees had fed there the day before, because the ground was littered with twigs and partly eaten fruit. Not wanting to disturb any chimpanzees, Goodall explained that she wanted to watch from farther away.

Adolf led them to a distant clearing directly opposite the msulula tree, with a good open space to watch. They waited and listened. Before long, Goodall heard the hooting of an approaching group of chimpanzees. As Goodall describes it,

> First one chimp gave a series of low resonant 'pant-hoots'—loud hooting calls connected by audible inhalations of breath. These grew louder and louder, until in the end the chimpanzee was almost screaming. Halfway through his calling another joined in, and then another.[3]

Soon the valley echoed with a wild chorus of pant-hoots.

The group approached through the forest behind the msulula tree, and the chimps followed each other, climbing up the palm trunk and disappearing into the branches. Goodall counted sixteen chimps, including a mother with an infant clinging to her stomach. The group fed on the fruit for several hours, but the foliage was too thick for her to see them. She caught only an occasional glimpse of a hairy black arm reaching out to pull in a bunch of fruit. Then, in complete silence, each chimp climbed down the tree trunk and disappeared into the forest.

Goodall searched the valley with her binoculars, hoping to see them climbing another tree, but to no avail.

For the next ten days, the msulula continued to bear fruit, chimps continued to come, and Goodall was there at her usual spot to watch. Adolf and Rashidi took turns accompanying her. For three nights they even slept there around a campfire, with Goodall wrapped in a blanket. She did not want to miss any early-rising chimps. Through binoculars, she observed every chimp movement and took detailed notes. Different groups came to this particular tree to feed. They came in groups of two or three or more. Some groups included males, females, and youngsters together, others were only adult males or females and youngsters. Always, however, the foliage was too thick to see any interaction between the individuals. Twice she tried to move closer, but as soon as the chimps saw her, they fled.

After ten days, Goodall and her scouts searched in other valleys for fruiting msulula trees but could find none. Nor could they find any more chimps. During the next eight weeks, they searched most of the twelve valleys of the reserve, trudging and crawling through dense undergrowth and climbing the ridges between valleys. Still they found no sign of chimpanzees.

Before she left for Gombe, wildlife researchers in both Nairobi and London had warned Goodall not to get her hopes up. They told her that chimps would never get used to human observers.[4] But she was not about to give up. She wondered if it was because there were three of them that the chimps seemed frightened. But even when Adolf and Rashidi watched Goodall from a peak as she traveled alone toward a group that she had seen in the distance, the chimps fled.

Although Jane Goodall initially wanted to roam the reserve alone, she had learned a lot from her scout companions. She learned to distinguish many of the animal tracks in the particular valleys where she would be working. She learned how to find her way through what seemed an impenetrable forest. In their daily wanderings, she had become familiar with many of the reserve inhabitants: bushbucks, bushpigs, mongooses, striped and spotted elephant shrews, and an assortment of rodents. She learned to distinguish the different varieties of primates in the Gombe Stream area. There were redtail monkeys, blue monkeys, an occasional silver monkey, large troops of red colobus monkeys, and even a few troops of vervet monkeys to remind her of those weeks on

Troops of olive baboons, similar to the one in this photo, were frequently seen. Some barked noisily until Goodall and her scouts finally moved out of sight.

Lolui Island. Most frequently seen were troops of olive baboons. Not all the baboons accepted the presence of humans. Some barked noisily and insistently until Goodall and her scouts would finally move out of sight. Only a few animals at Gombe were considered dangerous—mainly buffalo and leopards. But there were several kinds of poisonous snakes, including the puff adder, night adder, bush viper, spitting cobra, an eight-foot-long water cobra, and the deadly black mamba. Other hazards were scorpions and giant poisonous centipedes, which sometimes appeared in Goodall's tent, and during the rainy season there were mosquitoes and the ever-present threat of malaria.[5]

Goodall and one or both scouts went out searching for chimps every day. Each time, she learned her way around the area a bit more. Her skin became more hardened to the sharp-edged grasses and less sensitive to the bite of the tsetse fly and other tropical insects. She became more surefooted on the slippery slopes and more skillful at tramping through the rough undergrowth.

Jane Goodall was now prepared in every way for her study of chimpanzees, if only she could find them.

Discoveries

Jane Goodall had now been in Gombe almost three months, with only rare glimpses of the animals she had come to study. Dr. Leakey had warned her not to rush it, not to try getting close to the chimps too soon. Even so, she felt guilty about having nothing to report. "I'm letting you down," she wrote to Leakey. And he wrote back, "You can do it."[1] But there was also the worry that funding for her field study might run out before anything significant was accomplished.

About this time both Goodall and her mother fell seriously ill with malaria. They had been assured by the doctor in Kigoma that there were no malarial mosquitoes in the area, so they had not brought along the appropriate drugs. For nearly two weeks, they lay on their camp beds in their hot tent, sweating out the fever. They were too ill to travel the three hours by boat to see a doctor in Kigoma, so Dominic tended to their needs. When Mrs. Goodall wandered out of the tent one night in a delirium, it was Dominic who found her, unconscious, and helped her back to bed.

Goodall recovered sooner than her mother and was impatient to start work again. Still weak and not wanting her African scouts to see her in this condition, she started out alone one morning to climb the mountain that rose near their camp—the same one she had climbed on her first afternoon at Gombe. Along the way, Goodall had to stop several times to catch her breath. Eventually she reached an open peak and sat down on a large flat rock. The peak was about one thousand feet above the lake and offered a clear view of tree-filled Kakombe Valley below. Within about fifteen minutes, a slight movement on the slope below caught her attention. There, no more than eighty yards away, three chimps stood staring at her. Then they moved calmly out of sight into thicker vegetation. They had not fled in panic on seeing her. Could she have been right that the shy chimpanzees would be less fearful of one person alone?

Later that morning, much pant-hooting and screaming on the opposite mountain slope signaled the approach of more chimpanzees. Through her binoculars Goodall could see them come to feed on the fig trees growing along a stream in the valley. About twenty minutes later, another group moved across the same slope where she had seen the first three. Goodall could easily be seen on the peak. The chimps stopped and stared at her, then moved on a bit faster, but not in panic. Soon, with wild calling and swaying of branches, they joined the others quietly feeding in the fig trees below. Goodall took notes on everything she saw and watched intently for any sign of movement. When the chimps finally climbed down from the trees, they followed each other in an orderly line—adults, youngsters, and two small infants riding on their mothers' backs.

For Goodall, this was the best day she had had since her arrival at Gombe. Returning to camp that evening, she shared her excitement with her mother. Mrs. Goodall, who was still recovering from malaria, was much cheered by the news. Later, in referring to this long-awaited event, Goodall wrote, "That day, in fact, marked the turning point in my study."[2]

Every day for the next several weeks, Goodall returned to her peak. The fig trees growing in the valley below produced a bountiful crop of fruit, and chimps came every day to feed on the figs. Dressed obscurely in khaki campshirt and shorts and making no attempt to follow them, Goodall sat in full view on the peak. Her presence seemed to be accepted by the chimps passing on the slope below. Her new position seemed also to be accepted by her African scouts. Since they knew where she would be, there was no need for them to follow her.

Arising each morning at 5:30 to the sound of her alarm clock, Jane breakfasted on two slices of bread and a cup of coffee, then set off for a day of observing on the peak.

Some days she prepared to stay all night, carrying with her a small tin trunk in which were kept a kettle, coffee, tins of baked beans, a sweater, and a blanket. A tiny stream near the peak provided enough clear water for her needs. If she decided to stay all night, she sent word to her mother by way of whichever game scout climbed to the peak that evening to make sure she was all right.

Watching through binoculars and never trying to get close to the chimps while they fed in the trees, she began to learn about how they lived. Mostly they wandered about in small groups of four to eight, such as a mother with her children, or a group of males, or two or three groups joining together. The chimps Goodall observed seemed to be part of a community of about fifty chimps. After they finished eating and moved on, Goodall would slide down the mountainside, and collect samples of the leaves, flowers, and fruits she found to identify later. In this way she learned that chimps eat not only fruit but also many kinds of leaves, blossoms, seeds, and stems.

From her daily watching, Goodall caught an occasional glimpse of the chimps' social behavior. Once when a newly arriving female held her hand toward a large male in the group, he drew her hand close and pressed it to his lips. Goodall saw two adult chimps embrace each other in greeting, youngsters playfully chasing each other in treetops, and two infants pulling on a twig in a tug-of-war. Often after a long session of feeding, two or more adults sat under the trees grooming each other—looking closely over their companion's hair-covered body and removing twigs, dirt, insects, or whatever else was there. They appeared to need and enjoy physical contact. Sometimes, when one chimp had been grooming another, the groomer would stop and poke its companion, seeming to feel that it was his or her turn to be groomed.

Goodall also learned that chimps sleep in nests. On the evenings when they went to bed before dark, it was still light enough for her to see them making their nests. Except for infants who slept with their mothers, each chimp made its own nest every night. First the chimp chose an upright fork, crotch, or two firm, parallel tree branches. Then, bending smaller branches over this base and pressing them down firmly with its feet, the chimp gathered a handful of leafy twigs for a pillow and settled down for the night. In the morning, after the chimps had gone, Goodall would go to the trees, climb into those nests that weren't too high up, and examine them more closely. In some of the nests, the branches appeared to be interwoven, and all were clean of animal waste.

Meanwhile, Vanne Goodall, fully recovered from her illness, had set up a first-aid clinic for the local fishermen and their families. Under a thatched roof supported by four poles, she provided first aid with the medical supplies she had brought along—aspirin, Epsom salts, iodine, ointments, bandages, and cough syrup. One day, a very sick man with two deep ulcers on his swollen lower leg was brought to her. Mrs. Goodall urged him to go to the hospital in Kigoma. He refused to go, so she treated his wounds twice a day the best that she could. When after three weeks his

Chimps build nests in which to sleep. In the fork of a tree limb, they bend smaller branches over this base, press them down, and gather leafy twigs for a pillow.

leg was healed, word spread far and wide about the wonderful white-woman doctor. Soon many people with ailments were trudging for miles to reach the clinic. Mrs. Goodall's kind manner and her cures, which often worked, helped establish a feeling of goodwill toward her and her daughter. Their African neighbors had previously been suspicious of the two white women who were permitted to live on the reserve.

Five months after her arrival, Vanne Goodall had to return to England to manage things back home. The Kigoma government was no longer worried about Jane Goodall being alone on the Gombe Reserve, and the local inhabitants were now friendly. Before Mrs. Goodall's departure, Dr. Leakey sent his longtime worker Hassan to stay nearby. Both of the Goodalls were pleased to see again their friend from their days aboard his boat on Lake Victoria.[3] He would be a help around the campsite and would drive their balky motorboat to Kigoma each month to buy supplies and collect the mail.

Although Goodall missed her mother's companionship, she was now totally absorbed in her work.[4] After a long day of chimp watching, she would return to camp for a simple meal prepared by Dominic. She bathed in a small canvas tub supported by a wooden frame, in water that had been heated in a kettle over the campfire. Each evening by lantern light, she transferred that day's scribbled notes into more legible writing in her journal, while her only companion, a pet toad named Terry, gulped down insects drawn to the light. This ritual went on seven days a week.

From time to time, Europeans living in Kigoma invited Goodall to come for the weekend, but she always declined. They could not understand why "this young English girl living alone up the lake" would not welcome a couple of nights in a proper bed in a house. "They didn't realize," Goodall explained, "that chimps do interesting things on Saturdays and Sundays as well as any other day."[5]

Gradually the chimpanzees became less fearful of "this peculiar, white-skinned ape."[6] When she moved no closer than sixty to eighty yards and sat quite still, they continued with their feeding or grooming. Now, close enough to distinguish one from another, she gave them names. The first was Mr. McGregor, an old male whose hair was mostly gone from his head, neck, and shoulders. He reminded her of the old gardener in *The Tale of Peter Rabbit*. Then there was Flo, an old mother, easy to recognize because of her bulb-shaped nose and ragged ears. Her two-year-old daughter became Fifi, and her juvenile son, Figan. Flo often traveled with Olly, another old mother. Olly had a long face, and the fluff of hair on the back of her head reminded Goodall of her Aunt Olwen. Other chimps that Goodall knew by sight were David Graybeard, named for his silvery beard, and Goliath, who was not a giant as in the Bible but had an athlete's physique. David Graybeard was less fearful of Goodall than the other chimps were and seemed to have a calming influence on the group.

Before long, David Graybeard provided Goodall with an exciting discovery. Arriving on the peak one morning, she noticed a small group of chimps in the

As the chimps became less fearful of this "white-skinned ape," Goodall moved closer and sat quietly taking notes. The chimps continued with their grooming.

branches of a tree just below her. The male was holding what looked like pink flesh from which he pulled pieces with his teeth. Through binoculars Goodall could see a female and a youngster reaching out to his mouth. When the female picked up a piece of the pink object and put it in her mouth, Goodall saw that the object looked like meat. Soon a bushpig, with three small piglets, appeared under the tree, snorting and moving around. When Goodall moved closer, she could see that David Graybeard was the male in the tree, and he was eating a baby bushpig.

The chimps fed for three hours while she watched,

and when they finally climbed down, David carried away the carcass, followed by the others.

Jane Goodall had actually watched chimpanzees eat meat. This was a startling revelation. All along scientists had believed that chimps occasionally ate insects or small rodents, but that they were primarily vegetarians and fruit eaters. No one had imagined that chimps might kill and eat a mammal as large as a young bushpig.

One October morning, less than two weeks after the meat-eating observation, Goodall made another discovery. The rainy season had begun, and she was tired and wet from tramping through the valleys searching unsuccessfully for chimps. Suddenly she saw David Graybeard in the tall grass about sixty yards away. Through binoculars, she could see that he was squatting beside a mound of red earth—a termite nest. He poked a long stem of grass into a hole in the mound, withdrew it, and picked off the clinging insects with his lips. Goodall recognized that he was using the grass stem as a tool. David fed for an hour. When he wandered away, she approached the mound and poked one of his discarded stems into the mound. When she pulled it out, a number of termites were clinging to the stem. During the rainy season, these insects rise to just under the surface of the mound, preparing to emerge, and that is when the chimps feed on them.

About a week later, David returned to the mound with Goliath. Unbeknown to them, Goodall watched as they worked. They collected their tools—a firm piece of vine or several stems—scratched open a passage in the mound, and inserted the vine or stem to fish for termites. When a stem's end became bent, they used the other end or reached for a new one. Several times the chimps picked a small twig, stripped off the leaves, and used it as a fishing tool.

Goodall wrote detailed notes on what she had observed. This was the first recorded instance of a wild animal not only using a tool but altering an object so it could be used as a tool. Until that point, anthropologists believed that humans were the only tool-making animals.

Goodall immediately sent telegrams to Dr. Leakey about her two exciting discoveries—that chimpanzees eat meat and that chimpanzees make and use tools.

Regarding Leakey's reaction to these discoveries, she reported that "he was of course wildly enthusiastic."[7] There is little doubt that Goodall shared his enthusiasm.

Jane Goodall had learned much about our closest living relative. Her six-month grant was about to run out, but she was not about to stop.

More Discoveries

The news of Jane Goodall's two significant discoveries proved to be helpful in gaining further financial support for her field study. Before long, Dr. Leakey wrote to her from Nairobi that the National Geographic Society had agreed to grant funds so that she could continue her research.

In 1960 Gombe's rainy season began in October, bringing frequent thunderstorms with heavy rainfall. The grass grew to heights of six to twelve feet, the forest air was heavy with humidity, and the ground remained drenched. Chimp watching became difficult. The apes' movements were hidden by the tall grass, Goodall's binocular lenses were clouded with moisture, and strong winds whipped off the plastic cover meant to shield her from the rain.

During a downpour, the cold, wet chimps sat against a tree trunk or in their soggy nests, hunched up with heads bowed. In between rains, the group would trudge off in search of food.

Sometimes the roar of thunder and flashes of lightning seemed to challenge the adult males to display their strength. Goodall witnessed one of these "rain dances" from her spot on an opposite slope, where she had been watching a group of chimps feed in a large fig tree as dark clouds gathered. After two hours, the chimps climbed down and began their trek across the valley, when a sudden storm brought torrential rain and a resounding clap of thunder. Instantly one of the big males stood upright and began to pant-hoot louder and louder, while swaying rhythmically from one foot to the other. Then he charged about thirty yards down a slope, swung around a tree trunk, leaped into its low branches, and sat motionless.

At once, two other pant-hooting males charged after him—one breaking a tree branch and hurling it ahead of him, the other swaying branches of a tree back and forth at the end of his run. A fourth male also charged forward, leaped into a tree, tore off a large branch, and dragged it down the slope. Meanwhile, the females and youngsters had climbed into trees and sat watching the entire display. When the male who had started the performance climbed down from the tree and moved on, all the others quietly followed.[1]

As the rain-drenched months dragged on, the chimps began to grow irritable and almost hostile toward Goodall. If they saw her while on their way to feed, they often went elsewhere. One day when she was waiting on the side of a ravine, hoping chimps would come to feed at a fruit-laden tree on the opposite slope, she heard the footsteps of approaching chimpanzees. At once, she lay down flat under her rain cover. However, a large male chimp discovered her. He climbed into the tree directly above her, shook its branches, pounded the trunk, and screamed himself into a frenzied rage. Then he climbed down. Goodall could hear his footsteps behind her. He gave a loud bark, stamped the ground, and hit her on the head. Instantly, Goodall sat up. He stood looking at her for a long moment. Then he moved on, stopping often to turn and stare. One might think she would have felt shaken after this encounter, but not so. "There was a sense of triumph," she recalled. "I had made real contact with a wild chimpanzee. . . ."[2]

The rainy season did not end until June 1961. As the rains and heavy humidity lessened, so did the chimps' fear and hostility. Instead of watching from the peak, Goodall was now able to sit closer to the wild fig trees where the chimps fed each day. They had come to accept her as part of their surroundings.

Late in August, Goodall's sister, Judy, arrived from England. The National Geographic Society had wanted to send a professional photographer to take pictures for its magazine, but Goodall was reluctant to risk disturbing the chimps with the presence of a stranger. Instead she suggested to Dr. Leakey that her sister, Judy Goodall, who looked like her, come to Gombe to take some photos, and he agreed.

Unfortunately, the dry season ended earlier than usual, so rain was again a problem. Huddled under a plastic sheet with her photo equipment, Judy Goodall spent hours in the pouring rain, waiting for a glimpse of a chimp. Finally, on a few dry days in November, she did get some shots of Jane Goodall and the campsite, and she took the first-ever photos of the chimpanzees of Gombe.

In December the two sisters packed up the whole camp, tents and all, to be stored temporarily in Kigoma. They returned to England together, where Dr. Leakey had arranged for Jane Goodall to enroll at Cambridge University.

If the chimpanzee research of Jane Goodall was to be taken seriously in the science community, she would need academic credentials. Dr. Leakey had managed to get her admitted to Cambridge University to work toward a Ph.D. in ethology—the study of animal behavior. Although Goodall did not have the required bachelor's degree, she would be permitted to take several semesters of courses at Cambridge, and then submit a report of her chimpanzee study as a thesis for her Ph.D. (Doctor of Philosophy) degree.

From 1962 until 1965, her study of the chimpanzees at Gombe was interrupted each year by a winter semester at Cambridge. There she was told, over and over, that her methods of research were all wrong. In Goodall's reports on the chimpanzees, she did not begin with a theory to prove. Instead she wrote down what she saw and what she felt. She gave the chimpanzees names, not numbers. Her focus was on the individual.

Ethologists, on the other hand, were less personal in their studies. The animals being studied were regarded as stereotypes (similar), instead of thinking, feeling individuals. They were numbered, not named. Ethologists believed that numbers, measurements, and statistics would tell the scientific truth.[3]

Goodall listened to her advisors and their criticisms, but knew that she would return to Gombe, record observations in her notebook, and continue doing the research her way—naming the chimpanzees, and focusing on their individual differences.

After her first semester at Cambridge, Goodall was eager to return to Africa.[4] She wondered if the chimps would remember her, or if she would have to get them accustomed to her all over again.

On returning to Gombe, she found that the chimps seemed even more tolerant of her than before. One day, while Goodall was away from the campsite, David Graybeard ventured into camp and fed from the fruit on the palm tree shading her tent. When Dominic reported the incident that evening, it seemed unbelievable. The next morning, Goodall stayed in her tent typing the previous day's notes on the typewriter she had brought back from England. About mid-morning, David walked by the tent and climbed into the tree to feed. On leaving an hour later, he paused, looked into the tent, then wandered away. He came almost daily, and one time he went into the tent and snatched a banana from the table. Although Goodall was usually away taking notes, she

Chimps were often close enough for Goodall to make detailed observations right there in camp.

instructed Dominic to leave bananas out every day, in the hope that David would return. He did return, accompanied by Goliath and a chimp named William.

This was a welcome development. Now the chimps were close enough for Goodall to make detailed observations on the same individuals, right there in camp. She learned, through their social interaction, that Goliath was the alpha male—the highest ranking male chimpanzee in the area. He was the first to be greeted when a member of the group arrived to join the others. If William and Goliath reached for the same banana, William gave way to Goliath. William was timid. David Graybeard was calm and gentle, often quieting a frustrated or angry chimp with a few grooming strokes or by laying a hand on its body.

Goodall now agreed to allow a professional photographer to come to Gombe and take photos for the National Geographic Society. Dr. Leakey sent Hugo Van Lawick, a Dutch wildlife photographer. He was to film a documentary of chimp behavior for the society to use in preparing a film lecture for its members.

Van Lawick arrived in the fall of 1962. On the first morning, David Graybeard visited the campsite, ate his bananas, then pulled back the flap of the newly added tent. He stared at Van Lawick, who had remained inside, grunted and went on his way. Shortly after, Goliath and William arrived, and they, too, seemed undisturbed by Van Lawick's presence. Thus, he was able to get some excellent film of chimps greeting, grooming, and begging for food.

Van Lawick also needed to film other areas of chimpanzee life in the mountains and forests. With Goodall as his guide to possible sites, he lugged bulky camera equipment up and down mountain slopes, stumbled through tangled undergrowth, and sat for hours among biting ants and other insects, waiting for chimps. At the sound of his clicking movie cameras, the apes quickly disappeared, but within a month they became more accepting. He was able to capture on film such chimp activity as making tools, using tools at a termite mound, and battling an aggressive baboon, as well as other previously unphotographed behavior.

When Van Lawick left Gombe at the end of his assignment in November, Goodall was alone again.

With him, she had shared her love of both the chimpanzees and life in the wilderness. "In Hugo I knew I had found a kindred spirit—one who had a deep appreciation and understanding of animals. Small wonder that I missed him when he was gone."[5]

Shortly after Christmas, Goodall left Gombe for another term at Cambridge. During that winter, 1963, a documentary film for American television was proposed, featuring Jane Goodall and the wild chimpanzees. It would be sponsored by the National Geographic Society, and Dr. Leakey arranged for Hugo Van Lawick to go back to Gombe to film it. Following Goodall's second semester at Cambridge, she and Van Lawick returned to Gombe together.

Goodall focused much of her study now on Flo and her two youngest offspring—daughter Fifi, about three and a half years old, and son Figan, about eight and a half years old. Like David Greybeard and Goliath, they had become regular visitors to camp, as had several others seeking bananas. Their presence revealed much about chimp behavior for Goodall to record and for Van Lawick to film.

From Flo, Goodall learned that wild female chimps may have many mates, but they produce only one baby about every five years. Throughout a chimp's life, a strong bond exists between a mother and her offspring. Flo was an attentive, gentle mother and was the top-ranking (dominant) female in her chimpanzee community.

Adult males take no part in family life. They are the dominant sex, and the alpha male in a community bosses the others. Goliath was the alpha male at

Chimps make sponges. Above, Figan is licking moisture from leaves he has pushed into the water gathered in a tree hollow.

this time. He would reign for several years, until his strength and fierceness were overcome by another male—probably a younger one.

Goodall also discovered that chimps make sponges. They crush and chew leaves to make them more absorbent, then push them into tree hollows or rock crevices to soak up the water caught there. The chimps then remove the leaves and lick the water from them.

Chimps communicate with each other vocally. Unlike humans, they do not normally use their lips and tongues to form sounds, but they do have a wide range of different calls. Their hoots, pants, grunts, whimpers, barks, and screams are each specific to a given situation. For instance, they have calls for meeting another chimp, sighting food, or sensing danger.[6]

After her earlier discovery of chimps eating a baby bushpig, Goodall later discovered that chimps actually form hunting parties in which they set out to capture such game as monkeys and baby baboons.

Also, adult males often patrol the boundaries of their home territory and may attack unknown chimpanzees that invade their area.

Goodall was now using a tape recorder during her chimp watching, which eliminated the need to stop

Goodall began using a tape recorder during her chimp watching. Here she records the vocal sounds of an adult chimpanzee.

A curious little infant chimp reaches out to touch the hand of Jane Goodall.

observing to write down notes. Each day's recordings needed to be typed, and there were science reports to write and work to be done on her Ph.D. thesis. She would soon be needing an assistant.

During this time, Goodall wrote an article on her work at Gombe for *National Geographic* magazine, entitled "My Life Among Wild Chimpanzees." It was illustrated with photographs by Hugo Van Lawick. The August 1963 issue of the magazine, in which Goodall's article appeared, immediately sold out. Jane Goodall's work was now gaining public recognition.

Sharing Her Life

At the end of Goodall's third term at Cambridge in 1964, she and Van Lawick met in Washington, D.C., to present a film lecture on the chimpanzees of Gombe to members of the National Geographic Society. Melvin Payne, a member of the society, introduced Goodall as a lovely English lady who "traded her comfortable home in England for the primitive life of the African wilderness among the great apes."[1]

The image of this girlish-looking woman—in ponytail, camp shirt, and shorts—walking among the wild chimpanzees was an intriguing one. In 1964 an article in *The New York Times* said, "Fragile and blonde . . . she looks as if she should be pouring tea or watering the roses instead of prowling the bush."[2] This was the beginning of many lectures, articles, and books by Jane Goodall, on her own or in collaboration with Hugo Van Lawick. It was also the beginning of a more personal collaboration between Goodall and Van Lawick.

By the end of 1963, Goodall and Van Lawick had fallen in love. On the day after Christmas, while Goodall was at her family home in Bournemouth, she received a cable from Van Lawick asking her to marry him. They agreed to be married after her Cambridge term and their National Geographic Society lecture were over.

Returning to London, Jane Goodall and Hugo Van Lawick were married on March 28, 1964. Their wedding cake was crowned with a clay model of David Graybeard. Huge photos of David, Goliath, Flo, and other chimps decorated the walls at the reception. Yet their honeymoon was limited to only three days. Earlier, they had received a letter from Dominic, who was looking after the camp in their absence. Writing in Swahili, he announced that Flo had had a baby. This came as no surprise. The previous July, she had been seen being pursued by a number of adult male chimps. The newlyweds could not wait to return to Gombe to begin recording the development of this new infant.

They arrived back at their lakeside camp during a sudden tropical rainstorm. After stowing away their luggage, Van Lawick spied a rain-soaked Flo huddled in the fig tree across from their tent. When the rain stopped, he laid out some bananas, and Flo swung down from the tree, followed by Fifi and Figan. Cuddling the new baby to her chest, Flo walked on three limbs toward Van Lawick and Goodall. She took a banana and stayed there chewing on it while her tiny, hairless infant began to nurse. When the bananas were gone, the little family headed back to the mountains.

Goodall recorded this incident as "unforgettable; we were filled with amazement that a wild chimpanzee mother trusted us enough to bring her baby

Jane Goodall and Hugo Van Lawick, her husband, are visited by a curious monkey while setting up their photographic equipment at the Gombe Reserve.

close to us. . . . As soon as they vanished between the trees, Hugo and I danced around the tent pole."[3] They named the new baby Flint.

Soon after this event in 1964, they were joined by their first assistant, Edna Koning. The young Dutch woman had read Jane Goodall's first article in *National Geographic* magazine and made up her mind to come and work at Gombe. She took over the typing and helped in other ways. A second assistant, Sonia Ivey, arrived a few months later. She had worked as a secretary in England.

By the end of 1964, about forty-five chimps were visiting the camp in search of bananas. The Banana Club, as Goodall and Van Lawick called the gathering, was an ideal way to make observations of several individuals in one location, but the more timid chimps did not appear. A decision was made to move the camp away from the bustle of activity on the beach, where fishermen brought in nightly catches of dagaa (sardine-size fish) and spread them out to dry.

A spot on a ridge half a mile up the Kakombe Stream Valley was chosen. Here at Ridge Camp, they set up tents and brought the banana boxes. The chimps soon followed. This area was closer to their forest home, and they seemed more relaxed. The chimps were so relaxed that they began to make camp life difficult. Chimps have a fondness for chewing on cardboard and paper and sucking on cloth. No longer quite as fearful of humans, they entered the tents to search for and seize these items. Bedding and clothing had to be stored in wooden crates to avoid being stolen. One chimp even ran off with a full carton of groceries. A change would have to be made.

Earlier, in 1963, Goodall had conceived the idea of setting up a center for long-term, continuous research at Gombe. It would be a place where students working toward their graduate degrees could come and do field research. They could also take over whenever she had to be away. Van Lawick helped her work out the plans. With permission from the Tanzanian government, and funding from the National Geographic Society, the idea of a permanent research center began to take shape.

A site was chosen farther inland. Two sturdy buildings were constructed of aluminum siding on concrete foundations—a one-room structure for Goodall and Van Lawick, and a larger building with kitchen, workroom, and two bedrooms for the assistants. Thatching covered the roofs, and wire mesh covered the windows to prevent chimps from climbing in. A concrete banana storehouse was constructed in the valley below, to provide a feeding station for the chimps. Here it was possible for Goodall to regulate the frequency with which the chimps were fed, so as not to interfere with their normal search for ripe fruit.

Early in 1965, Goodall and Van Lawick left for England, where Goodall worked on her Ph.D. dissertation, entitled "Behavior of the Free-Ranging Chimpanzee," and Van Lawick began editing a film for the National Geographic Society. In December, Goodall was awarded a Doctor of Philosophy degree in ethology. She is only the eighth person in the history

At the feeding station, the older chimps sometimes take more than their share. Above, six-year-old Fifi checks to see if Goodall might have hidden her banana ration.

of Cambridge University to have received a Ph.D. without first earning an undergraduate degree.

When Goodall and Van Lawick returned to Gombe in 1966, they encountered an alarming situation. Olly's four-week-old baby became the first victim of a polio epidemic. The paralyzing disease had begun with an outbreak of polio among Africans in a nearby village. Chimpanzees are susceptible to many human infectious diseases. Possibly a chimp had contracted the polio virus while roaming near the village, and it then spread to those in the Gombe community. Goodall was then pregnant. Neither she nor Van Lawick had received a full course of polio vaccine. They immediately contacted Dr. Leakey by radio telephone. He arranged for Pfizer Laboratories in Nairobi to fly oral polio vaccine to Gombe for Goodall, Van Lawick, their staff, and the chimps. Vaccine, hidden in bananas, was administered to the chimps—three drops once a month for three months. For some, it was too late. Polio claimed the lives of six chimpanzees in the group, including Mr. McGregor.

Later that year, a number of graduate and undergraduate students applied for field study at Gombe, and several more buildings were added in which to house them. The students put in hours and hours of observation and added much to the understanding of chimpanzees. Some also studied baboon and red colobus behavior. The research community became officially known as the Gombe Stream Research Center, with Dr. Jane Goodall supervising the students' work, and Van Lawick handling the administrative details.

In 1967, Hugo Eric Louis Van Lawick was born. Goodall called his birth "the most important event of my life."[4] Van Lawick and Goodall originally nick-named their son Grublin after a chimp infant, but it was soon shortened to Grub.[5] As he grew older, he became known as Hugo to all except family and close friends. While he was small, Goodall gave up working with the chimps, and students took over the daily observations.

Grub was guarded very carefully. Wild chim-panzees are hunters. Several years before Goodall arrived, they had taken two African babies for food. When Grub began to walk, his parents built a second house on the beach, with a caged-in porch where he could play safely. If he played on the beach, two African nannies watched over him.

In the mornings Goodall worked in her office at the beach house—writing reports and science articles and advising students. The rest of the day she spent with Grub—reading to him, taking him for walks (in a sling on her back, when he was an infant), and teaching him about creatures of the forest. As he grew older, he had lessons every morning with a tutor. Grub was a blond, outgoing child. He learned to speak Swahili along with English, and he had many playmates among the children of the African staff.

Goodall and Grub often accompanied Van Lawick in his Land Rover to his camp in the Serengeti. Here he was filming a documentary and writing a book on wild African dogs. These wild dogs roam in packs for miles across the plains. They hunt such animals as gazelle, wildebeest, and zebra and eat them alive.

As time went on, Van Lawick's safaris to photograph and film documentaries of wild animals took him great distances, and he was gone from Gombe for long stretches of time. Goodall needed to spend most of her time at Gombe, in work related to her chimpanzee research. Eventually they were apart more and more. In 1973 they finally agreed to divorce. They stayed good friends, however, and often worked on projects together. "We don't feel any bitterness," Goodall has said. "We had a jolly good time and produced Grub. We achieved together more than we could have done separately."[6]

Up until this point, Goodall's research had revealed that although chimpanzees were excitable, they were basically peaceful beings. During the next few years, however, she was to see their darker side.

The chimpanzees of Gombe live in at least three territorial communities—identified by the names of valleys in their ranging area. The central group is known as the Kasakela community, the group Goodall had been studying near the Gombe Stream Research Center. The northern group is known as the Mitumba community, and the southern group is the Kahama community. The latter was named by student researchers in 1972, when they discovered a new group of chimps.

The Kahama community, comprising six males and three females, had broken off from the original Kasakela community and established itself in a new territory to the south. Adult males from the Kasakela community set out on raids to murder the members of the southern group. One such raid was recorded in February 1975, in which Goliath (who had joined the Kahama group) was brutally attacked and fatally beaten.

By early 1970, through her *National Geographic* articles (which were illustrated with Van Lawick's photos) and the television documentary, Jane Goodall had become known around the world as a leading primatologist. Beginning in 1970, she spent three months each year as a visiting professor at Stanford University in California and was honorary visiting professor of zoology in 1972 at the University of Dar Es Salaam in Tanzania.

In 1972 Goodall joined a group of researchers en route to Dar es Salaam to ask the government to designate Gombe as a national park. The director of Tanzania's wildlife parks was Derek Bryceson who, like Goodall, wanted to protect wildlife. He was very much in favor of Goodall's idea, and through his efforts, Gombe Stream Game Reserve became Gombe Stream National Park.

Before Goodall met him, Bryceson had been a longtime member of Tanzania's parliament, from which he had recently resigned. Goodall and Bryceson fell in love, and they married in 1974.

Derek Bryceson had been a member of the Royal Air Force during World War II. At the age of nineteen he suffered a spinal injury when his plane was shot down. Told he would never walk again, he taught himself to move about with a walking stick. He learned to drive a car and to fly his four-seater airplane, in which he made periodic visits to Gombe, where Goodall continued to live.

On May 19, 1975, forty armed rebels crossed the lake from Zaire and kidnapped four Gombe students. A week later, one of the kidnapped students was sent back to the Tanzanian government with demands of a cash ransom and the release of rebel party leaders from Tanzanian jails. The rebels threatened to kill the hostages if their demands were not met. Goodall and the other researchers escaped to Bryceson's house in Dar es Salaam, where they waited anxiously for news of the three remaining hostages. The crisis was finally resolved in July, and the hostages were released.

The possibility of more terrorist kidnappings prompted the government to immediately ban non-Tanzanians from working in Gombe. This included Jane Goodall. A special police force was sent to patrol the area. Only those staff members who were Tanzanians were permitted to return to the research center.

Since Goodall was not permitted to return to Gombe, she remained with her husband in Dar es Salaam. Meanwhile, her Tanzanian field assistants collected data on chimp behavior and reported their findings to her.

The following month, another episode of chimpanzee violence was discovered. Passion and Pom (mother and daughter chimps) were killing and eating infants born in the Kasakela community. For the next three years, only one infant escaped these cannibalistic attacks. Finally, in 1977, Passion bore a baby of her own, and the killings stopped. Goodall named the baby Pax, which is Latin for peace.[7]

When she was finally permitted to return to Gombe for a few days a month, drastic changes needed to be made in research procedure. The Tanzanian field assistants, originally employed to accompany students unfamiliar with the African bush, would now have to be trained to carry on the research themselves. With help from Derek, who was fluent in Swahili, Goodall taught the staff about collecting data, making charts and maps, and writing reports. Since that time, most of the research data have been collected by Tanzanian field assistants, with Goodall checking the reliability of the reports.

Goodall now lived mostly with Derek in Dar es Salaam but made frequent visits to Gombe. Grub, who had continued studying with a tutor, was now ready to enter school in England. He would stay with his grandmother and return to Africa for holidays and summers. Life became more relaxed for Goodall. She and Derek often took vacations together, flying in his plane or boating and fishing near their home. Whenever apart, they talked daily by radio-telephone, and he continued to help Goodall with many of Gombe's administrative chores.

After five years of marriage, Bryceson became ill with cancer. Hoping for a miracle cure, he sought treatment at a clinic in West Germany, with his wife staying nearby. In the fall of 1980, Bryceson's heroic battle ended with his death.

Goodall was devastated by the loss.[8] Her friends

speak of her marriage to Bryceson as having been "a real love match."[9] She returned to their home in Dar es Salaam, where her family members and their many friends shared her sorrow.

In time, Jane Goodall would gather the strength and the will to carry on with her work.

9

Another Dream

When Louis Leakey sent Jane Goodall to Gombe in 1960 to study wild chimpanzees, he warned her that the study might take ten years. Goodall laughed and thought "maybe three."[1] Now, decades later, chimpanzee research at the Gombe Stream Research Center is the longest field study of animals in the world.

Since 1975 most of the observations continue to be done by trained Tanzanian field assistants supervised by two deputies and one administrative officer, with Dr. Jane Goodall as the scientific director. In addition to chimpanzee research, studies are also being done on baboons and colobus monkeys.

Jane Goodall's methods of research, once

ridiculed as unscientific, are now used by other ethologists and have become the standard against which other observation techniques are measured.[2]

Praise for her chimpanzee field study has come from many scientists, including Dr. David Hamburg, professor at the Stanford University School of Medicine, who wrote:

> *This study is unique in the history of research on animal behavior . . . because individual animals have been recognized and studied in all their individuality, because rich, close-range observations are accurately recorded, . . . because the individual animals have been studied in the context of their own community, . . . and because the study has in all respects been conducted with great care and integrity.*[3]

Dr. Roger Fouts, a psychologist who studies sign language in chimps, has said, "She let the chimpanzees tell her about themselves. Her life is a progression of discovery after discovery."[4]

Goodall spends less time at Gombe in the 1990s, because of her travels around the globe giving interviews and lectures on behalf of chimpanzees. Her schedule has included African countries (Uganda, Burundi, Congo, and Tanzania), the United States, Canada, Mexico, Europe, and Japan. She speaks at scientific conferences, universities, schools, museums, zoos, and wherever people will gather to listen. Although her purpose is to educate us about the behavior of chimpanzees, she also focuses on the perils facing our closest living relatives: mainly, our encroachment on their natural habitat, and the need

Here, Jane Goodall speaks at the National Press Club in Washington, D.C., on behalf of the World Wildlife Fund. Her fund-raising lectures to save the earth's primates keep her constantly on the go.

for more humane treatment of those chimps in captivity.

All across the chimpanzee range in Africa, their natural home territory is disappearing. The chimpanzee range covers a wide belt, which extends across equatorial Africa from the west coast to within about one hundred miles of the east coast. As the human population increases, it needs more land for housing and for growing food. And so, forests are uprooted, the land cleared, and the wild chimpanzees lose their natural shelter and food source. This creates social stress, which, if unrelieved, can lead to breeding failure and the eventual extinction of these great apes.

Gombe National Park, home to about one hundred and sixty chimps, is protected by the Tanzanian government. However, with the forests around the area cut down, Gombe resembles an island surrounded by housing and cultivated land.

Another threat to chimpanzees is poaching—the illegal hunting of these primates. In 1990 there were about one hundred and seventy-five thousand chimps left in the world. The number keeps decreasing, which is due, in large part, to poaching. In some countries in west and central Africa, adult chimps are killed for food. Baby chimps are sold as pets within Africa, or they are sold to dealers who send them abroad for use by entertainment or medical research industries.

Because mother chimps are very protective of their infants, the mothers are shot, chased with packs of dogs, or poisoned by hunters, and the babies captured and sold. Goodall tells of the distress suffered by an infant whose mother has been shot:

> *A little chimp in the wild is always with the mother. The child will stay near the body of its mother, keep going back, listening for the heartbeat. They have the same emotional attachment to their mothers, the same need for reassurance, the same insecurities as we do.*[5]

Many young chimps are smuggled into the resort areas of Spain or the Canary Islands. Here they are drugged to keep them quiet, dressed in baby clothes, and their thumbed feet are crammed into tiny shoes. Then they are paraded around the tourists, led by roving photographers hoping to attract customers who would like to be photographed with a young chimp. Others are trained to perform in nightclubs, circuses, and movies, often through the use of force. Young chimps frequently are beaten by impatient trainers. A blackjack rolled inside a newspaper, to disguise it from human onlookers, can bring instant obedience from a performing chimp.[6]

In many countries, including the United States, there is a market for baby chimpanzees as pets. Jane Goodall feels that chimps are not suitable as pets. In an interview with Joan Lunden on ABC-TV's *Good Morning America*, Goodall explained, "When they become adolescent, they're potentially dangerous, four times stronger than us. They don't want to be disciplined. What do you do with them then? They go into the labs, into the circuses, into the zoos."[7]

A chimpanzee ending up in a medical laboratory is

subject to another form of animal abuse. Because chimps are genetically so like humans, they make ideal stand-ins for scientists to use in trying to learn more about human diseases. Chimps can be infected with diseases to which other animals are resistant, such as acquired immune deficiency syndrome (AIDS) and hepatitis, and then studied.

Goodall recognizes the value of chimps as research subjects. It is the way they are treated by those who use them that she finds "shockingly cruel."[8] A few years ago, while visiting a lab in Rockville, Maryland, near our nation's capital, she saw room after room of small, bare cages in which chimps sat huddled in despair. Young chimps, two together, were crammed into cages so tiny they could barely turn around. At least they had each other for comfort, at the moment. But they would soon be infected with hepatitis, AIDS, or influenza and placed in cages by themselves, each cage enclosed in an isolette—a steel box with one tiny window.

> I watched one of these older chimpanzees, a juvenile female, as she rocked from side to side, sealed off from the outside world inside her metal isolation chamber. . . . When she was lifted out by one of the technicians . . . she sat in his arms like a rag doll, listless, apathetic. I shall be haunted forever by her eyes, and the eyes of the other chimpanzees I saw that day.[9]

Goodall hopes her efforts to reveal these inhumane conditions will lead to finding other methods for animal research. Meanwhile, she has suggested ways in which the suffering of chimps can be reduced: using larger cages, exposing chimps to the outdoors, and allowing them more contact with other chimps so they can play and groom each other. Also, providing toys and video games would help to relieve their boredom.

Many research laboratories, including the one in Rockville, Maryland, are beginning to follow her suggestions. Spacious new cubicles have been built for the chimps, with glass walls, sleeping platforms, climbing equipment, and toys. Kept in pairs, the chimps can now see one another through the walls and play with lab workers, sometimes pressing their backs against the glass for a pretend scratch. "When they moved into the new enclosures, their personalities changed. I could see it," said executive John Landon.[10]

The conditions in zoos have also been a concern to Goodall. The Jane Goodall Institute has established Chimpanzoo, a research program to create more public awareness. Using the same observation methods that Goodall used at Gombe, students gather and analyze data on chimpanzee behavior in captivity. The results are then added to Jane Goodall's long-term study of chimps in the wild.

The Jane Goodall Institute for Wildlife Research, Education, and Conservation, established in 1977, supports four major programs: the Gombe Stream Research Center, the study of chimps living in zoos (Chimpanzoo), improvement of conditions for chimps being used in medical research laboratories, and conservation activities such as establishing sanctuaries for the protection of orphaned chimpanzees in various African countries.

Roots and Shoots is another program offered by the Jane Goodall Institute. A worldwide awareness program, its purpose is to encourage young people to respect and care for their environment, animals, and fellow human beings.

Financial support for the institute comes from private donations, contributions, grants from corporations, and the royalties received from Jane Goodall's lectures, documentary films, and the many books she has written for both adults and children. Some of the titles include *My Life with the Chimpanzees*; *Grub: The Bush Baby*; *My Friends: The Wild Chimpanzees*; *In the Shadow of Man*; and others.

During Jane Goodall's 1986 visit, she and a chimpanzee observed each other at Chicago's Lincoln Park Zoo.

In 1986 Jane Goodall became spokesperson for the Committee for the Conservation and Care of Chimpanzees. This group of scientists lobbied legislators in Washington, D.C., to list chimpanzees as an endangered species and to provide legislation ensuring the well-being of chimps that are confined in laboratories and zoos.

Jane Goodall is a member of the American Academy of Arts and Sciences and has been the recipient of many awards. Among them are conservation awards from the San Diego Zoological Society, the New York Zoological Society, and the J. Paul Getty Wildlife Conservation Prize. Also, she received several awards from the National Geographic Society, including its most prestigious honor, the Hubbard Medal, for her groundbreaking work with chimpanzees.

Of all her achievements, perhaps the one that gives her the greatest joy is her son, Hugo. Now an adult, he is handsome, articulate, and adventurous. He sometimes travels with his mother, once appearing with her on Phil Donahue's television talk show. He also spends time at his father's tent camp on the Serengeti, accompanying him on photographing safaris. An expert swimmer and fisherman, skills he developed during his childhood on the Lake Tanganyika shore, he has his own commercial fishing business in Tanzania. In her book *My Life with the Chimpanzees*, Goodall wrote, "Suppose someone else asks me: 'What have you contributed to the world?'" She would answer, "Well, I have raised a wonderful son."[11]

Even in her sixties, Goodall still wears her

graying blond hair in a youthful ponytail, and her dedication to the chimps—their welfare and that of other animals—is as strong as ever. Her fund-raising lectures keep her constantly on the go. "During the past nine years," she says, "the longest I've spent in any one place has been three weeks."[12]

And where might she spend those few weeks? She could go to her childhood home at Bournemouth, where her mother and her Aunt Olly live. Or she could return to her home in Dar es Salaam, which holds so many memories of her late husband. It is quite likely that part of the time, she will be six hundred and seventy-five miles west of Dar es Salaam, trekking through the rain forest of Gombe for a reunion with Fifi, her family, and the other chimps. "In that environment," she once said, "with the chimps around me, I find the spiritual strength to battle in the States."[13]

Recently Jane Goodall gave a lecture at Cornell University—an event that had been sold out for weeks. Later she sat at a table in the crowded lobby, signing copies of her books. "Follow your dreams,"[14] she wrote in each book.

Many years ago, Jane Goodall's dream of working with animals in Africa came true. She has lived most of her life in that way. But now it seems she has another dream—that of teaching all of us to respect chimpanzees, and other animals, as we should respect each other.

With her effort and ours, perhaps that dream, too, will come true.

Chronology

1934—Born in London, England, on April 3. *Jubilee* (handwritten)

1939—Family moves to Bournemouth, England.

1940—Attends Uplands School, near Bournemouth.
-1952

1952—Attends secretarial school in London; works as secretary and as assistant film editor.

1957—First trip to Africa; works as assistant secretary to Dr. Louis S. B. Leakey, anthropologist and curator of National Museum of Natural History, Nairobi, Kenya.

1959—Returns to England; works as film librarian while waiting for financial backing for her chimpanzee project in Tanzania.

1960—Returns to Africa; begins her study of chimpanzees in Gombe Stream Game Reserve, Tanzania.

1962—Studies toward Ph.D. degree, one term each
-1965 winter, at Cambridge University; awarded Doctor of Philosophy degree in Ethology.

1964—Marries Hugo Van Lawick, wild animal photographer for *National Geographic* magazine; administrator of chimpanzee project at Gombe.

1967—Son Hugo Eric Louis Van Lawick (nicknamed Grub) is born; Goodall writes *My Friends the Wild Chimpanzees* (with Hugo Van Lawick).

1970—Visiting professor of psychiatry and human
–1975 biology at Stanford University.

1970—Writes *Innocent Killers* (with Hugo Van
Lawick).

1971—Writes *In the Shadow of Man.*

1972—Writes *Grub: The Bush Baby* (with Hugo Van
Lawick); honorary visiting professor of zoology, University of Dar Es Salaam, Tanzania;
member of American Academy of Arts and
Sciences (honorary foreign member).

1973—Goodall and Van Lawick divorce.

1974—Marries Derek Bryceson.

1977—Establishes Jane Goodall Institute for Wildlife
Research, Education, and Conservation.

1980—Derek Bryceson dies of cancer.

1984—Receives J. Paul Getty Wildlife Conservation
Prize.

1986—Spokesperson on Committee for the
Conservation and Care of Chimpanzees.

1987—Is awarded the R. R. Hawkins Award from
Association of American Publishers, for *The
Chimpanzees of Gombe: Patterns of Behavior.*

1988—Writes *My Life with the Chimpanzees.*

1990—Scientific director of the Gombe Stream
Research Center; writes *Through a Window:
My Thirty Years with the Chimpanzees of
Gombe.*

1993—Writes *Visions of Caliban* with Dale Peterson.

1995—Is awarded Hubbard Medal by National Geographic Society.

1996—Is presented with Lifetime Achievement Award from National Alliance for Animals; is awarded the Medal of Mount Kilimanjaro, the highest honor from Tanzania.

Chapter Notes

Chapter 1

1. "So Like Us," Jane Goodall interview with Sam Donaldson, *ABC News Primetime Live*, aired November 23, 1993.

2. Jane Goodall, *My Life with the Chimpanzees* (New York: Pocket Books, 1988), p. 70.

Chapter 2

1. Alex Chadwick, *Weekend Edition Saturday*, National Public Radio, Transcript #1122, May 6, 1995.

2. Ibid.

3. Ibid.

4. Timothy Green, *The Restless Spirit, Profiles in Adventure* (New York: Walker, 1970), p. 9.

5. Jane Goodall, *My Life with the Chimpanzees* (New York: Pocket Books, 1988), p. 20.

6. Ibid., p. 22.

Chapter 3

1. David Collins and Peter M. Gareffa, "Jane Goodall," in *Newsmakers* (Detroit: Gale Research, 1991), p. 146.

2. Jane Goodall, *My Life with the Chimpanzees*, National Geographic Video, 1990.

3. Martha E. Kendall, *For the Love of Chimps* (St. Petersburg, Fla: Worthington Press, 1995), p. 36.

4. Ron Arias, "Jane Goodall," *People*, May 14, 1990, p. 97.

5. National Geographic Video, 1990.

6. Peter M. Gareffa, "Jane Goodall," *Contemporary Authors* (Detroit: Gale Research, 1981), Vol. 2, p. 261.

Chapter 4

1. *Gombe 30 Commemorative Magazine* (Tucson: The Jane Goodall Institute, 1991), p. 24.

2. Ibid.

3. Tess Lemmon and John Butler, *Apes* (New York: Ticknow & Fields, 1993), pp. 8, 9, 16.

4. "Jane Goodall," *Current Biography Yearbook 1991* (New York: H. W. Wilson, 1991), p. 250.

5. Jane Goodall, *In the Shadow of Man*, rev. ed. (Boston: Houghton Mifflin, 1988), p. 12.

Chapter 5

1. Ron Arias, "Jane Goodall," *People*, May 14, 1990, p. 97

2. Jane Goodall, *In the Shadow of Man* (Boston: Houghton Mifflin, 1971), p. 16.

3. Ibid., p. 19.

4. Sy Montgomery, *Walking with the Great Apes* (New York: Houghton Mifflin, 1991), p. 94.

5. Jane Goodall, *The Chimpanzees of Gombe: Patterns of Behavior* (Cambridge: Harvard University Press, 1986), pp. 50-51.

Chapter 6

1. Timothy Green, *The Restless Spirit* (New York: Walker, 1970), p. 21.

2. *Gombe 30 Commemorative Magazine* (Tucson: The Jane Goodall Institute, 1991), p. 14.

3. Jane Goodall, *In the Shadow of Man*, rev. ed. (Boston: Houghton Mifflin, 1988), p. 50.

4. *Gombe 30 Commemorative Magazine*, p. 10.

5. Green, p. 24.

6. "Jane Goodall," *Current Biography Yearbook 1991* (New York: H. W. Wilson, 1991), p. 250.

7. *Gombe 30 Commemorative Magazine*, p. 16.

Chapter 7

1. Jane Goodall, "My Life Among Wild Chimpanzees," *National Geographic*, August 1963, pp. 302-303.

2. Jane Goodall, *In the Shadow of Man*, rev. ed. (Boston: Houghton Mifflin, 1988), p. 59.

3. Sy Montgomery, *Walking with the Great Apes* (Boston: Houghton Mifflin, 1991), p. 102.

4. Martha E. Kendall, *For the Love of Chimps* (St. Petersburg, Fla: Worthington Press, 1995), p. 62.

5. Goodall, *In the Shadow of Man*, p. 75.

6. Aline Amon, *Reading, Writing, Chattering Chimps* (New York: Atheneum, 1975), p. 21.

Chapter 8

1. Sy Montgomery, *Walking with the Great Apes* (Boston: Houghton Mifflin, 1991), p. 109.

2. 1964 article in *The New York Times*, cited on "So Like Us," Jane Goodall television interview with Sam Donaldson, *ABC News Primetime Live*, aired November 25, 1993.

3. Jane Van Lawick-Goodall, "New Discoveries Among Africa's Chimpanzees," *National Geographic*, December 1965, p. 804.

4. Jane Goodall, *My Life with the Chimpanzees* (New York: Pocket Books, 1988), p. 76.

5. Phil Donahue interview with Jane Goodall/Hugo Van Lawick, TV Transcript #042988, 1988.

6. Mary Virginia Fox, *Jane Goodall: Living Chimp Style* (Minneapolis: Dillon Press, 1981), p. 41.

7. Montgomery, p. 124.

8. Peter Miller, "Crusading for Chimps and Humans . . . Jane Goodall," *National Geographic*, December 1995, p. 114.

9. Miller, p. 114.

Chapter 9

1. Peter Miller, "Crusading for Chimps and Humans . . . Jane Goodall," *National Geographic*, December 1995, p. 110.

2. "Jane Goodall," *Current Biography Yearbook 1991* (New York: H. W. Wilson, 1991), p. 252.

3. David A. Hamburg, M.D., Foreword to *In the Shadow of Man*, rev. ed., by Jane Goodall (Boston: Houghton Mifflin, 1988), p. x.

4. Ron Arias, "Jane Goodall," *People*, May 14, 1990, p. 99.

5. David Collins and Peter M. Gareffa, "Jane Goodall," *Newsmakers* (Detroit: Gale Research, 1991), p. 148.

6. Jane Goodall, "Chimps in Peril," *Gombe 30 Commemorative Magazine* (Tucson: The Jane Goodall Institute, 1981), p. 35.

7. Joan Lunden, "Status of Chimpanzees," ABC-TV's *Good Morning America*, Transcript No. 1771, March 29, 1993.

8. Goodall, p. 35.

9. Ibid., pp. 36-37.

10. Miller, p. 127.

11. Jane Goodall, *My Life with the Chimpanzees* (New York: Pocket Books, 1988), p. 108.

12. Miller, p. 116.

13. Sy Montgomery, *Walking with the Great Apes* (Boston: Houghton Mifflin, 1991), p. 212.

14. Miller, p. 122.

Further Reading

Goodall, Jane. *Grub: The Bush Baby.* (Photographs by Hugo Van Lawick.) Boston: Houghton Mifflin, 1972.

———. *The Chimpanzee Family Book.* Saxonville, MA: Picture Book Studio, 1989.

———. *The Chimpanzees of Gombe: Patterns of Behavior.* Cambridge: Harvard University, 1986.

———. *In the Shadow of Man.* Boston: Houghton Mifflin, 1988. Original edition published under name Jane Van Lawick-Goodall, 1971.

———. *My Life with the Chimpanzees.* New York: Pocket Books, 1988.

———. *Through A Window: My Thirty Years with the Chimpanzees of Gombe.* Boston: Houghton Mifflin, 1990.

Green, Timothy. *The Restless Spirit: Profiles in Adventure.* New York: Walker, 1970.

Montgomery, Sy. *Walking with the Great Apes: Jane Goodall, Dian Fossey, Birute Galdikas.* New York: Houghton Mifflin, 1991.

Nichols, Michael. *The Great Apes: Between Two Worlds.* Washington, D.C.: National Geographic Society, 1993.

Peterson, Dale, and Jane Goodall. *Visions of Caliban.* New York: Houghton Mifflin, 1993.

Van Lawick-Goodall, Jane. *My Friends: The Wild Chimpanzees.* Washington, D.C.: National Geographic Society, 1967.

• • • • •

The Jane Goodall Institute, P.O. Box 599, Ridgefield, Connecticut 06877, (203) 431-2099.
Internet: http://www.wcsu.ctstateu.edu/cyberchimp/

Index